SEXY JOKES and SEXY SAYINGS

TOO SEXY FOR THIS BOOK

Bojan Milosevic

SEXY JOKES AND SEXY SAYINGS

Too Sexy For This Book

Copyright © Bojan Milosevic, 2023

ISBN: 978-0-6456776-7-6 Paperback

ISBN: 978-0-6456776-8-3 E-book

First published 2023

All rights reserved. Without limiting the rights under copyright reserved above, no part of this publication may be reproduced, stored in or introduced into a database and retrieval system or transmitted in any form or by any means (electronic, mechanical, photocopying, recording or otherwise) without the prior written permission of the owner of the copyright.

SEXY JOKES
Too Sexy For This Book

If you keep it above the belt, I will listen to any story you share. It's not difficult to impress me.

It's a dog's world when my owner brushes me – reasons the dog. I never trouble the dog with bad news.

Good luck with it all. I hope all your dreams come true.

Great men get married to Lady Luck because what a lucky man indeed.

It's for me, not for you, but if you feel like sharing. There is more for everyone when it's on the table on offer.

He, he, he many laughs when you cannot smile anymore.

Why smile if you can kiss?

Do you want me to kiss you – a – hello?
Customs and traditions and all that,
that's why!

You don't just blow up a balloon; you need
a party in town. Let me know what's on
the cards!

If you show me your cards, I will show you
mine. Aces are aces, and jokers are jokers. So
these cards are about poker.

Do you feel like playing poker?
I will play poker under one condition!
We play strip poker.
Otherwise, strip tease, then poker!

Why play games when we could get serious?

By the way, how's your love life?
Are you happy or not?
Tell me why about being happy or not.
If you're unhappy or otherwise happy, that

would mean you want some love. The scales are tipped in favour of the love side of life.

Which is your favourite cheek to kiss?
Let's kiss three times for good luck.
Note that the third kiss is on the lips.

So, do you enjoy more? Then, tell me more, please. Otherwise, I will say, "more, please more"!

I told you to tell me any story you want and keep it above the belt but do not whisper sweet nothings!

Are you free for coffee?
Yes, OK!

Will it be your place or mine?
That's where all your dreams come true!
Until then, let me know along the way. Do you dream of me? Let me know all about you and me. I need to know how much you want me!

If you want me, you can have me!

Just kiss me quickly.

If your husband catches you in the act with me, tell him we are kissing cousins. He's only my cousin. How sweet. He's the innocent type.

Why do you say I need to pass the gullible test?
Because nobody knows my love for you.

How do you really get to know a lady?
Let me know, please!

What does it take to win you 'over'?

More than one kiss means love.
Are you in love with me, or do you need some more?
Yes or no, please!

OK, I've got that…
Is it going to be your place or mine?

Is it true it takes two to be in love?
It takes two to be in love, but three is company.
More than that could be - let's throw in the towel and have a party.

Sometimes I tell corny jokes, but this time it's horny ones.
Are you sexy, fun or enjoyable? Otherwise, say all of the above!
It ticks every box above.

Can I have your phone number?
Do you want mine?

Your eyes are so beautiful, sexy, and horny; they tell me a lot. You seem to feel so moist and wet that if there was a wet T-shirt competition... you would be great on my lap for a wet underwear dream!

Are you into wet dreams?
To find out, let's take a seat on the lounge, and you sit on my lap.

Now living on the streets.
She drove me out.

For more, saucy and creamy and all that.
Otherwise, the meat market is where
dating happens.

Making a deal, take your cut in it. Do you
play poker or not? Let's deal. Let's play cards,
strip poker or strip tease.

The joker card is not part of the game.

How much sex does it take to be sexy?
It's ongoing.

If she's on top, when is she caught
from behind?

Two is company, and three is a crowd. But a
foursome is not for all; it's only for some.

Twist, poke and be not awake. Dreamin',
Dreaming of her.

She's a glamour. Does that mean everyone knows she's famous!

She's not a virgin!

Jumbo, jumble in the jungle. Hairs and all.

Let's beat around the bush.

Shave it, and the saying is, let's not beat around the bush.

Ferrari, Porsche, limousines and pink Cadillac, all about living in the fast lane.

She's made for herself pillow talk.
Hot rods are on her lips.

Careless whispers.

She's doing it now. Wow!

About my hot rod on her lips.

It's got to be big; this song was made for me!

Baby Jane, in the back lane.

Don't give it to me, aha, aha, because me, myself, and I, are coming after you instead.

Me, myself and I, three ways to refer to me. All about me.

Do you want to dance, because soon the DJ is going to 'rock da House'. All about house parties.

Who knows who's who in the zoo?
Are you a R – apist. Apes are on, hehe.

You belong in the zoo was the Nineteen eighties commercial.
Can it come back on TV again about how it was, and how it should be. Personal request.

Apex, time, control, quality and management. All about management principles.
Ape – x – Go for it.
Time – after midnight, when no one sees.
Control – she's all nuts.

Quality – not quantity.
Management – let's go crazy.

Keep Australia beautiful and put the rubbish in the bin. I request can all the old commercials about me be placed on TV again. Solo man (solo the drink), XXXX beers, and the lot keep it traditional.

Mello Yellow was a great soft drink; bringing it back is a great request.

Sex management, Bachelor.

Sex problems, there's too much going on!

Sex therapy, please help!

The 'X' Factor, Why? Because Y and Z are too late for the talent factor.

Does a zoo keep its animals free?
No, because you have to pay an entry fee to see them!

Does it all work out for you?
Only if she's in love.

Does love make sense?
Sensuality is all about love .

Do people root around?
Only if they miss the plug-hole. I miss her so much!

Does blind Freddy see problems?
Yes, even blind Freddy can. So, what about you? So, what!

Does sex turn her on?
Yes, when she flips over!
Does Flipper the dolphin laugh?
Only for TV. What a Star!

Do people love hamburgers?
Only if they are treated well. What a great hamburger!

Does a hamburger bite back?
No, it only gets eaten up, he, he.

CONTENTS

FORWARD v

INTRODUCTION vii

SEXY JOKES   Too Sexy For This Book 1

Jokes from around the World 25

Conclusion 29

FORWARD

Hi everyone, and what a great book I have prepared for you.

By the way, I have much excitement built up in this forthcoming joke book with sexy sayings to tickle you pink. To show you how talented I am, to come up with a book so gifted as this one.

I will explain a little about myself. I was born in Camperdown in Sydney, NSW, Australia, in King George V Memorial Hospital. I completed two tertiary courses: an Associate Diploma in Civil Engineering from 1992 to 1994 and a Bachelor of Building Degree from 1995 to 1998.

Throughout my career, I was employed as a Ground Test Technician and have worked in the Building Industry, where I was involved in Contracts Administration work. During my life, I have matured nicely and developed some excellent speaking abilities in all sorts of facets.

This joke book was challenging to write because it is about my personal jokes that I have never heard.

I have decided that I am willing to be a book writer on a broad spectrum, and part of my dream involves getting involved in a joke book such as this. I have sketched other joke books and have to type them up, but this one is a classic for your pleasure. So get your eyes stuck into this book, knock your socks off being pleased, and find it your pleasant little paradise to laugh with me in all this. I hope you are willing to have many laughs and possibly you may use some of these jokes in life to find yourselves friends and the like.

INTRODUCTION

This book is a gem of jokes and sexy sayings that make people laugh. I wrote this book to prove that I can write a funny book that will sell and convince people that I am an interesting character who can please everyone when they read some of the various books I will write for the public.

Along the way, I want to make it a beyond-doubt issue that I have established myself as I continue writing more books. Another reason I wrote this book is that, along with you, the beautiful reader, I look forward to sneaking up on people to do with this joke book. I plan to have a great laugh, and you are my target. I can only imagine your smile when you listen to some of this, as I use it on people.

Let's make it our customs or traditions to make interest factor out of these sayings, and I welcome the media or any famous organisation to spin off these sayings. However, my gain is making my book famous for people to buy it. If people are willing to accept my book, it makes people laugh and could make your day much more comforting during life's trials. Since happiness is what people seek everywhere, then let this book bring you there. Laughs, tears of joy and many smiles are what it is all about. So use it on your friends.

All the best.

Do you find me your 'dream man'?

Wet dreams for us.

I was dreaming of you all night.

Can I tickle your fancy?
Only if you say so!

Otherwise, you may want more than that.
Is it true?
Sometimes!
Kind Of!

Have you got the hots for me?
Please come; I Love you. Let me hold your hand and make you come!

Are you willing to come, or should I rub you up now?

Smooth sailing or hot rods, what
are you into?

Which one do you have?

Obviously, not a yacht!

So, do you like it fast and all that?

A hot rod, then!
To fish you in, I need to take the plunge!

That's above the belt when you keep the belt above one leg.
What happened to the other leg?

Leg spreads are only for horny chicks!
Let's spread some cream excitement.

Are you a screamer, or do you shout?

Let me know what you say when you are this loud!

Oh, Oh, I love you!

Is that all?

Nope, but it's embarrassing to tell all!
Then it's our secret!

Please tell me; otherwise, I may need to work on you.

If you yell more, more, I will get it! Does it sound like your style?

Friday, Saturday, night fever. Are you hot and horny? Does it get steamy?

To be satisfied, we need to place a big wet patch on the bed sheets tonight.
Is it your bed or mine?

Only if you feel like going for it.

All about sex, all about now. Are you going to miss out or not?

It's now or never. So hold on and let me take you there.

Are you a workaholic? About me, I happen to be handy right now! It's all hands on.

Let's get it off. I don't believe in clothing right now, what about you?

Let's not believe in clothes. So why not smile?

All about smiles. Up, down or around the back. How revealing, about vertical smiles.

The more smiles, the more there is to know. All you have to do is smile, if you get my drift.

How much fun can you have in one night?
About satisfied smiling, Ahh, is that it!
If you're not satisfied, why smile then?

Seriously, it's only showing off, not smiles, when you get serious about it all.

Vertically or horizontally speaking, unless you get surprised when you see it's round.

When planning ahead: all considerations are welcome.

If you are unsure what to make of it, make of it all you can; even round, not only horizontal or vertical, could work.

Big tits are where it fits. If you are out of your mind, you could have the fits.

That's why ladies have a fit if they have not been getting any.

Anywhere will do, wherever I get laid.

That's why it's hen's night to make sure the rooster has a friend.

There are the birds, the bees, hens and roosters, or rooters and hooters. Nobody is interested in halftime. Play on!

Softball, baseball, bat-on balls and all.

The hat on your cock proves you are no softy!

Have you heard the Joe Cocker song about how you can leave your 'hat on' when your clothes come off? A rock 'n' roll song!

Bad whispers mean she is keeping secrets; her husband is around the corner.

If she screams, that means that she is yours!

About divorce, it could be a lot of yelling!

Not a lucky husband, she does whisper.

She's into monogamy.

Polygamy works like this: Poly wants a cracker; she wants a cock or two.

Manipulating her is enough. More is required to make it with her. She's fresh, exciting, so exciting to me.
So, what's the answer?

Claim your stake all about the meat market.

Your place or mine?

About a Steak House.
Then stakeout.

Does dumbo the elephant have a long trunk?
What else does he have?

Does a dog bark? Yell, laugh or play!
A dog can imagine a yell in its mind after it hears one for up to one hour.
Do you agree with me?

Living animals can have the same mind as a person but cannot talk or speak. They know what they see, but their reasoning is wild sometimes because they cannot talk or speak. Sometimes people act absurdly also.

For example, the dog bites but a person rapes and murders. Have you ever put some thought into this?

Does Lois Lane love superman?

No! She only loves Clark Kent!

Superman screwed up in the telephone box dress-up! A suit on him looks better as Clark Kent. If money doesn't buy love Superman can only have a fling with Lois Lane as she flies off in his arms. He he!

Do you go to Australia Zoo? To which clan do you belong? Support Australia Zoo, are you one of us? Queensland – Australia.

Does TV turn you on?
Do you turn on the TV?
She's sexy, and always on TV. That's why!
There's always a reason to turn on the TV.

Do people fool around?
Only when they have a lot of living to do.
What a fool! Many laughs.

Do you not know that Kentucky Fried Chicken is hot and spicy?
That's because it's better than going Cold Turkey.

Does Madonna sing?
Only a song!

Do you care for a root?
Money is the root of evil.

Do black ladies love the cock?
Yes, oh yes, oh yes!

Does Tarzan love Jane?
Only in the forest.

Do the freemasons have a forest lodge?
Tarzan and Jane also happen to be members there.

Let's love the freemasons at – Forest Lodge.
The Bermuda Triangle – all about her hairy bush.

How many 'Wacken Farries' are there in life?
It's not fair.

Do you have secret affairs?
Yes, not out in the open!
Secrets behind closed doors.
When you leave home, all people know the lot. He he.

How much is a Quarter Pounder from McDonald's?
A Quarter of a pound. Drugs, sex, rock 'n' roll and a Quarter of a pounder.

Don't smoke—only lick.

Cock smoko and cunt licking, far out, man. I only lick. I have never done any smoko. All the best about all you do. Enjoy!
Wacko tobacco, the best smoko!

Cunt smoke, all about quarter-pounders!

Do you hate, love or enjoy sex?
Or is it pleasure and pain?

I heard on TV that Aids, HIV, Hepatitis A, B, C, Cholesterol and diabetes are not true. It has been discovered. What great news!

Does a train trip unless it goes on and on.
How long are the train tracks?
Not half a length. Obviously.

Unlike the old freemason saying how long is a piece of string, half a length. Knowledge travels a long way these days about the crazy freemasons. Choo choo, chew.

Cannibalism, not cannon ball-ism.

If you live far away, I hope you get home before your shoes wear out.

A train with a flat tyre.

It still gets to you, I know. Many laughs.

A shoe lace per shoe, like lace for a lady. What would she do without shoes? He he.

Does it rain now?
Buckets full.

'Mad' is the biggest saying on earth. How 'Mad' – that's 'mad'.

It's all over, how about that?

Sloppy seconds not even for a minute!
That's enough to do you in.

A break for freedom; virginity sucks.

Black cats, tigers, cheetahs and robbers.

Regarding cheating in life, black cats are said to have nine lives. What cheats!

Does pussy pink or love machine stink? Only down the sink. Otherwise, do the plunge into the other hole.

Does pubic hair need to be curly? Grab by the short and curlies and find out.

The straight and narrow always stands out.

Does sex become a flunk? Only if she's not a hunk!

Hero's come and go, but blind bats do not! The blind bat is better than the hero; in other words, it gets to stay!

Heroes have friends, but Scott-no-friends does not seem to be a hero!

Caps and baseball hats are not cool. It can lead to baldness. Why? It suffocates hair. Some advice from me!

Beanies are not different. Watch out, please.

Do not drink and drive.

When crossing the road, look out.

When driving, do not speed.

Love, sex and marriage 'Rules'!

    The End of my personal section

Jokes from around the World

What did the toaster say to the slice of bread? "I want you inside me."

"Give it to me! Give it to me!" she yelled. "I'm so wet, give it to me now!"

She could scream all she wanted, but I was keeping the umbrella.

Two men broke into a drugstore and stole all the Viagra.

The police put out an alert to be on the lookout for the two hardened criminals.

They say that during sex you burn off as many calories as running eight miles. Who the hell runs eight miles in 30 seconds?

Why do walruses love a Tupperware party?
They're always on the lookout for a tight seal.

I'll admit it, I have a tremendous sex drive.
My girlfriend lives 40 miles away.

Who's the most popular guy at the nudist colony?
The one who can carry a cup of coffee in each hand and a dozen donuts.

What's the difference between kinky and perverted?
Kinky is when you tickle your girlfriend with a feather, perverted is when you use the whole bird.

A woman walks out of the shower, winks at her boyfriend, and says, "Honey, I shaved myself down there. Do you know what that means?"
The boyfriend says, "Yeah, it means the drain is clogged again."

How do you make a pool table laugh?
Tickle its balls.

If you were born in September, it's pretty safe to assume that your parents started their new year with a bang.

What do tofu and dildos have in common?
They are both meat substitutes.

How is playing bridge similar to sex?
If you don't have a good partner, you better have a good hand.

What do you get when you jingle Santa's balls?
A white Christmas.

Why isn't there a pregnant Barbie doll?
Ken came in another box.

What's the difference between a sex worker and a drug dealer?
A sex worker could wash her crack and resell it.

What are the three shortest words in the English language?
"Is it in?"

What did the hurricane say to the coconut tree?
"Hold on to your nuts, this ain't no ordinary blow job!"

Conclusion

This book has been a handy little gem, and I expect it will sell like hotcakes. I enjoy how this book can double up as a sexy pick-up lines guide for the sexually frustrated who are interested.

If you think this book is too sexy for your friend, do not give it away. Keep it for a rainy day when sex liaisons are on your mind and you need to get some. Get some, get-go and get on with it.

All the best, and warning everyone, many jokes ahead, so take care!

www.ingramcontent.com/pod-product-compliance
Lightning Source LLC
Chambersburg PA
CBHW040244010526
44107CB00065B/2869